The Book You Must Read Before You Turn 40!

Real-Life Lessons About Relationships, Boundaries, and Becoming Who You Actually Are — Without the Fluff

By

Hope Genero & René Shanti

ISBN: 979-8-9937706-1-1
First Edition, 2025

Written from Two Voices — Sometimes Aligned, Sometimes Hilariously Not.

And yes… even if you've blown past forty, it still applies.

Table of Contents

Fabulous Forty

Why is forty more than just a number between thirty-nine and forty-one?

For us, it's a symbol. We're not talking about a midlife crisis, gray hairs, or our bodies falling apart—though some of that did happen. We're talking about a season of life when everything shifts—and you, like us, will be completely unprepared for the craziness that follows.

And honestly, it doesn't have to land exactly on your fortieth birthday. For most of us, it's a season, not a number—a stretch of life where things finally click into focus.

It's the moment when you suddenly start seeing yourself clearly—often for the first time.

And that clarity?

It doesn't appear out of nowhere.

It shows up after years of searching, collecting experiences, surviving things you never signed up for, and finally being willing to unpack what's been sitting in the back of your emotional closet.

Those pieces come through reflection, honesty, and the willingness to address uncomfortable things. But if you're willing to look, the clarity that follows can be both grounding and life-changing.

That's actually why we wrote this book—and we probably should say this right up front.

We're not psychologists or self-help experts. We're two women who have lived a lot of life together, learned the hard way, supported each other through things we could have never predicted at nineteen, and eventually realized something important:

No one tells you what your thirties are really preparing you for.
And no one prepares you for forty at all.

So we decided to tell you.

With you in mind, we structured this book in short, bite-sized chapters you can read while you're hiding in the bathroom, waiting in a school pickup line, or stealing five minutes for yourself. Most pieces are light and easy to digest, but some dive into deeper places—the walls we built, the baggage we avoided, the beliefs we inherited, and the tools we eventually learned to use.

Our hope is that through our experiences, you'll begin to recognize the patterns, beliefs, and habits that may be quietly steering your life—sometimes in directions you never consciously chose or want.

Some topics we both take on, and you'll see very quickly that our perspectives can be wildly different. That's intentional. Sometimes one of us will speak to you more clearly than the other. Sometimes both angles together paint a picture you didn't know you needed.

And don't be surprised (even though I'm telling you this now—you will be surprised) when something jumps out and slaps you in the face—emotionally, lovingly, and usually at the worst possible moment.

We've left space for you to catch that. You don't have to write anything profound. Just write what's true.

If you decide to read this again later, some things will likely hit differently—because you'll be different. There's space for that too.

We hope you do come back to this someday, and when you do, you might decide to thank your past self for these changes.

We hope somewhere in these pages you find at least one piece that feels like your piece—the one that helps you understand something about yourself that you've been carrying for years without realizing it.

And now that you know why we wrote this, it's time to meet the women behind these pages.

We tell our stories through Greek goddess names. Each of us chose the goddess who best represents the other. You'll see each "goddess" at the top of her section. We each have our own stories, our own wounds, and our own wildly different perspectives. So let's start with the one whose journey of "strength" wasn't at all what it appeared to be.

Athena

I'm Athena. My friends chose this name for me because Athena is known as the goddess of war, courage, and strength. I'm extremely flattered that these traits come to mind when they think of me.

Unlike the real Greek goddess, I've struggled with plenty in life—and my Achilles' heel has always been relationships. On the surface, I'm great at socializing, having fun, and generally being well-liked. But deep, meaningful relationships? Not so much. I've been told I can come across as intimidating—all five-foot-three inches of me—which I still find amusing.

What I didn't realize was that those same traits—confidence, independence, competence—also made perfect bricks for the walls I built around myself long before I ever understood they were walls.

People have always described me as strong, but what they saw wasn't strength. It was protection. Being strong enough to overcome obstacles is not the same as living behind armored defenses. Everything you're about to read comes from lessons learned in the school of hard knocks.

I want to share my struggles because before I began my journey of truly understanding myself, I had no idea the level of love I've now found even existed. I've worked hard to improve my relationships and to understand people from a new perspective, and the results have been life changing. These chapters are pieces of my puzzle—stories about walls I built, hurts I avoided, beliefs I inherited, and the tools I used to untangle it all.

I hope you relate to one of us and that somewhere in these pages, you'll find at least one small piece of your own puzzle that helps you continue your journey.

You've heard my side. Now it's time for Hestia's—and trust me, her take is a whole different experience in the best way.

Hestia

Let me introduce myself. I am Hestia. Hestia is the goddess of hearth, home, and domestic life. She is a caretaker—as am I.

I am a daughter, a friend, a wife, a mother... and a hot mess. Honestly, I wanted to write this book to let anyone else out there like me know that you don't have to feel like the Lone Ranger.

Over the past ten years, I've learned more about myself than I ever imagined there was to know. Now that I'm 45 and looking back, I wouldn't go back. I really like me now. I understand myself in a way I never could have expected. Through reading a great deal, journaling a little, and talking to my besties a lot, I finally got to this place.

Life served me a trauma buffet as a kid. I survived sexual trauma, abusive boyfriends, toxic family relationships, and life-altering loss. Not only did I survive all that, I made lemonade from those rotten apples. Please know that I'll talk about working through my trauma, but never in graphic detail—only enough to explain how I eventually found peace.

I am an extremely empathetic person. An empath can intuit the emotions of the people around them, and I was born with that ability. I describe it like a car radio: as the car moves, nearby frequencies make contact. If the radio is tuned in, it picks up the signal. Sometimes it even picks up multiple signals at once. That's how empathy works. Some of us have a very sensitive receiver. My empathy was confusing when I was young. It took years of practice to decode those transmissions, but now I value the insight they give me. To someone with a low level of empathy, it may seem confusing—but Athena offers a great explanation later in the Tool Shed.

I am also an introvert who doesn't naturally seek out new people or open up easily. Don't get me wrong—I am personable. If approached, I will talk to almost anyone (with exceptions, as you'll read in "Be a Rhino!"). But I need quiet, alone time to recharge. Extroverts build energy through interaction; I build mine through solitude.

I love being a mom more than almost anything. I married an amazing man who feels like my other half in nearly every way. In the wise words of my favorite philosopher, Deadpool, his crazy matches my crazy. I can say with complete certainty that I wouldn't be where I am in my growth journey without his support and encouragement.

I have three amazing kids. I'm constantly amazed at how much I love them—and then amazed all over again the next day when I somehow love them even more.

I also have best friends who have been my besties since high school. One of them is Athena. They are kind, smart, giving, hilarious, supportive, loyal, fierce, and absolutely amazing bitches.

My hope for this book is to let you know that there is always more to learn about ourselves. The beautiful thing about being human is that we are capable of growth throughout our entire lives. I no longer find that frightening. I'm excited about who I might become tomorrow. I hope our insights and epiphanies help someone out there—or, at the very least, make you feel less alone.

Most likely, one day you'll wake up, look around, and think, How the hell did I get here?

We did too.

So we went back—way back—to trace how it all started.

And like a lot of people our age, everything pointed in the same direction:

The Plan.

The Plan – Everybody's Doing It!

(Athena)

Of the three of us best friends who've known each other for more than twenty years, two of us have been divorced—and those divorces happened for very different reasons. But strangely enough, they both began the exact same way: with The Plan.

Not our plan.

The Plan.

The script so many of us follow without even realizing we're following it.

Graduate high school.

Go to college.

Date someone responsible.

Build a future.
Check the boxes.

I didn't question any of it. I just lined up behind whoever seemed to have their life together and followed right along.

Looking back, I can see exactly how it happened—and exactly why it didn't work.

I married at nineteen. People told me I was too young, which of course only made me more determined to prove them wrong. I truly didn't understand what age had to do with anything. In my mind, I was basically a seasoned adult: I had a job, a car, and a whole year of living at home while paying one bill. Clearly, I was qualified to make lifelong decisions.

And for a while, it looked like I was right. We built a very stable life. We raised kids. We checked every single box. But deep down, I knew I would never find true happiness in that relationship. I chose him for many good reasons—just not the right one. He wasn't "the one," and I knew that early on.

So why did I go through with The Plan anyway?

Because I honestly believed there wasn't a "one" for me.

After my divorce, I finally asked myself a question I had dodged for decades:

Why do I believe in soulmates… but not for myself?

The answer surprised me:

I didn't think anyone could understand me deeply enough to actually be my soulmate.

Have you heard the song "Bitch" by Meredith Brooks?

Yeah. That's me.

I'm a walking contradiction in the best way—and sometimes in the most confusing ways. And for years, I believed no one would ever "get" me enough to choose me fully. So I chose someone safe, someone good, someone "good enough." A lot of us do that; we just don't call it that at the time.

And here's what I couldn't see back then:

I wasn't able to recognize what was right for me because I didn't know myself well enough to see it.

Those older, wiser people who raised an eyebrow at nineteen-year-old me?

Turns out they weren't wrong.

But it wasn't the number that mattered—it was what I didn't know yet.

Sure, I knew my personality, my style, my politics, my religion.

But I did not know:

What I needed

What I couldn't compromise

What actually made me happy

How my childhood shaped my choices

How my fears influenced my relationships

Or why I kept choosing safety over connection

All the foundational pieces—the ones that actually determine the success of a relationship—didn't click into place until after my divorce.

And here's the part I wish I had known at nineteen:

Self-knowledge comes before soulmates.

You cannot find what you truly need when you don't even know what you're looking for.

If The Plan feels familiar, you're in good company—most of us have lived some version of it. I'm the one who cannonballs straight into the deep end, no hesitation. Hestia, though? She's the type to dip a toe in, feel the water, and think, Hmm, maybe this isn't quite my thing.

Our approaches couldn't be more different—and that contrast is exactly what helped both of us see our own patterns more clearly.

The Plan... What a Crock! (Hestia)

I've always envied the way Athena charges full steam ahead into whatever she wants. It hasn't always worked out, but for years I thought nothing ever phased her. As we grew older and our friendship deepened, I realized neither of our approaches was ideal. Back then, we didn't understand it, but I needed her to push me to be bolder, and she needed me to slow her down and make her think. Even with all my careful decision-making, life still managed to throw punches I never saw coming. What I didn't realize then was that those punches weren't unique to me.

At some point, everyone finds themselves in a relationship that feels like a sweater you didn't realize you'd put on backward. It's uncomfortable, restrictive, and just... not quite right.

Let me start here: when I was in high school, I took all the right classes, earned great grades, and graduated with an Academic Honors Diploma. According to The Plan, that's how you get into a great school. I followed The Plan and was accepted to a great school. Then reality hit: paying for that great school. Not enough financial aid, no credit, and suddenly—slap in the face. End of the road.

I was a good kid. I worked hard. I got terrific grades. I followed The Plan. How is it feasible that college is now out of reach?

I was deflated. My future was a complete unknown. College was always The Plan. That plan was supposed to get me far away from my nightmare of a childhood.

How was it possible that I'd followed The Plan and somehow ended up completely off track—with no idea how I got there or how to get back? That's when I learned The Plan is complete fiction.

At twenty-one, I was fully embracing being twenty-one. Most of my friends were away at college. Athena was both married and in college. I had a good-paying job, a crew to party with, and no responsibilities beyond rent and my car payment. Then I met a guy.

He was the life of the party—generous, always buying drinks, hilarious, constantly cracking jokes or doing impressions that had everyone in stitches. If there was fun to be had, we were going to find it. Isn't that what I was supposed to do at twenty-one? Before I knew it, I was pregnant.

A baby? Another slap in the face.

Most of our relatives decided we had to get married. I was still trying to wrap my head around going from shots and jokes at the bar to being Mom and Dad. I needed a break.

To appease everyone, we got engaged. Deep down, though, I knew the relationship didn't feel right. I didn't have the language yet to understand that the "off" feeling was the absence of emotional fulfillment. Eventually, I convinced myself the relatives might be right—that a truly fulfilling relationship was as rare as a unicorn.

The pressure was on to set a wedding date. They wanted us to follow The Plan—the same mythical plan I'd already learned was fiction.

I began to question happiness. Could I make myself happy if I married him?

I wanted my baby to be happy. But how could I teach happiness when I hadn't figured it out myself? As I sat with that question, I realized the version of me who was engaged was not the same version who had started that relationship.

She had different priorities, spent her time differently, and—most importantly—had entirely different goals.

I was angry and frustrated. My fiancé and I disagreed about everything: household chores, finances, child-rearing, and the general direction of our lives.

I was depressed, stressed, lonely, and misunderstood.

Do I stay in this relationship?
Maybe one day we will be different.
What if we agreed on handling our finances?
Is there any way we could ever be happy together?
Don't we deserve to be happy?
What does a happy couple look like?
Should we end it?
Does he love the real me?
Is this the real me?
What can I do?

I didn't like that version of me.

Neither of us were at our best, and I could only see one way that we might be able to find happiness: I had to break off the engagement.

Dealing with the relatives' emotional reactions was almost as hard as the decision itself. I was the "bad guy." And that's a tough place to be when you're certain you're doing the right thing.

Eventually, we both met the people we were actually meant to be with. Sometimes the "bad guy" is exactly who you need to be. Sometimes the bad guy is actually the person who is courageous enough to say the difficult thing that needs to be said.

Don't be afraid to step into that role when it's necessary. In retrospect, I'm grateful I had the strength to do the extremely unpopular, cripplingly painful, ultimately right thing.

I can't offer step-by-step instructions for navigating a situation like this, but I can say this: the most important thing is to know yourself. I knew, with absolute certainty, that I wasn't the best version of me. I would encourage anyone in a relationship they have serious doubts about to take the time to figure out who you've become—and who you want to be. Read everything you can get your hands on. Most importantly, if you need a break, give yourself one.

Take that sweater off, turn it around, and get on with your life.

Once we finally understood how we wound up
on this path, we started questioning
everything—especially our relationships.

The ones we chose.

And the ones that chose us.

Toxic Is Toxic
(Hestia)

My granddad used to say, "You can polish a turd, but it'll still stink—so don't waste your time."

There are situations in life where the most effective course of action is simply to move on. When I picture a healthy partnership, both people care equally about their own happiness and the happiness of the person they love. When we hear the term toxic relationship, most people immediately think of romance—but the truth is, when a person is toxic, every relationship they touch has the potential to become toxic. That includes relationships with family members.

To have a healthy relationship of any kind, I believe there must be communication, understanding, respect, and boundaries. A family relationship is no different. Without those things, I struggled to create them in other areas of my life.

Breaking free from toxic behaviors isn't easy. The key for me was recognizing the happiness factor. If I'm constantly expected to choose between my happiness and someone else's, that relationship may be toxic.

I found myself in one of those relationships—with someone I couldn't exactly break up with. It was a precarious position to be in. Ultimately, Athena helped me see it clearly—without guilt or pity.

When I had my first child, I was not in a fulfilling romantic relationship. One of my family members made plans nearly every weekend and counted on me to participate.

In the beginning, I went along just to get time away from my "baby daddy." It was fun for a minute, but damn.

At some point, I became utterly exhausted by my entire weekend consisting of a sprint to handle grocery shopping, bill paying, laundry, and all the event attendance.

The turning point came on a Saturday when I was on the way out the door. An unmistakable aroma reached my nose. My son had a dirty diaper.

Damn it. Back into the house.

With an armload of a diaper bag, purse, sippy cup, stuffy, and of course, the baby, I unlocked the front door. Instead of unpacking the diaper bag, I decided to change him in the nursery. Just as I laid him down, I heard the landline ring in the other room. Are you kidding me?

Back in the Stone Age, our only phones were attached to the house, so I grabbed a clean diaper, a pack of wipes, the diaper bag, my purse, the sippy cup, the stuffy, and of course, the baby, and headed toward my bedroom, where the phone was. I scrambled to the bed, laid him down, and grabbed the landline.

I cradled the phone with my shoulder while removing the stinky diaper. On the line, I heard—

"Why are you still at home!?"

"What do you want?" I said.

"When are you leaving?"

"In a minute!" I fumed.

"What are you doing?"

"The baby shit!"

I hung up the phone and finished the diaper change. Then I grabbed the diaper bag, purse, sippy cup, stuffy, and of course, the baby, and headed for the door.

When we arrived at the event, I was unloading the car when someone grabbed my son from the back seat. From behind me, I heard the usual chorus of jeers about my lateness.

Someone called out, "What happened to you?"

My 21-month-old son yelled, "I shit!"

I turned toward him, stunned. That moment slapped me in the face. I had been talking about him, in front of him, like he didn't understand me. I felt embarrassed, misguided, and completely unqualified to be responsible for this tiny human. I was so wrapped up in this weekly sprint that he became another item I dragged along instead of my priority.

No more.

Now, when I consider requests for my time, I think in terms of three rules I try to apply to myself.

Rule #1: Choose Happiness

This rule applies to everyone—family, friends, and coworkers. I shouldn't be expected to prioritize the happiness of anyone who doesn't do the same for me.

Rule #2: Respect Boundaries and Refuse Guilt

I don't make demands, hold unrealistic expectations, use pity or guilt to get my way, or cross boundaries—and I'm entitled to expect the same in return.

Pity, in particular, has been used against me by someone I loved. I was manipulated into believing I was responsible for their happiness. Whenever they perceived a wrong or disappointment, the solution was for me to fix it—by doing something, buying something, or sacrificing something.

If a person adopts a dog from a shelter who has only one good eye, they might feel sorry for it. The dog senses that weakness and assumes leadership over the "weak" human. The dynamic is the same when pity is used as manipulation—it shifts power and creates imbalance.

Once I realized what was happening—and how this person repeatedly hurt me while feeling entitled to do so—I had no choice but to create distance. And I learned something essential: it's perfectly acceptable to distance yourself from an unhealthy relationship, no matter who it's with. Finding the perfect amount of distance in order to have an enjoyable relationship is a dance. That dance proved to be both illuminating and enriching for me.

Rule #3: Feelings Are Not Accusations

My feelings are just that—mine. They're not right or wrong, and they're not accusations. They're messages that deserve to be acknowledged and understood. If I ignore them or push them down, they don't disappear—they turn into resentment.

Over time, I learned something that changed everything: if I base my happiness on someone else's actions, I hand them control over my life.

I choose instead to let myself feel what I feel without giving anyone power to dictate my emotions. I no longer accept responsibility for other people's happiness.

That doesn't mean I don't love them—it means I refuse to participate in unhealthy dynamics. I move forward as the keeper of my own happiness.

Because toxic is toxic, no matter who it's coming from. And learning to recognize it has saved me from a lifetime of turd-polishing.

Your Turn

What idea from these topics stayed with you longer than the others?

If you want to write:

What felt familiar?

What felt uncomfortable?

We figured out that difficult relationships come in all varieties.

So, to figure out which relationships are helping us become the people we want to be, we have to move forward instinctively.

Be a Rhino!
(Hestia)

One morning long, long ago, I rolled out of bed—footie pajamas and all—and sashayed into the living room to climb into my granddad's recliner with him. He looked at me and asked, "Did you get your eyes together last night?"

I didn't look up. "Yep."

"How'd you get 'em over your nose?" he chuckled at his own joke.

He had lots of sayings like that—things I didn't understand as a kid. He repeated them often enough that I memorized many without even trying. At the time, I definitely did not see value in them. As I grew up, they took on new meaning. He was quietly teaching me lessons I wouldn't fully appreciate until adulthood.

One thing he told me over and over was that the real me is who I am when no one is watching. I didn't get it back then, but now I see how wise he was—and how lucky I was to have him.

Who a person truly is at heart is reflected in the choices they make when no one is looking—when there can be no repercussions, positive or negative. The choices a person makes in solitude are indicative of that person's character. That truth reflects itself in the energy they emit.

In the animal world, there are predators who hunt for food and prey animals who forage. Both are essential. "Predator" in nature isn't a moral judgment—it's simply one part of a balanced ecosystem.

I believe the human world isn't all that different. Some people, knowingly or unknowingly, target those whose insecurities make them easier to manipulate. In quiet moments of interaction, people radiate an energy that reflects who they are. If you quiet your mind and pay attention, you can learn to read it.

My empathy and insecurity made me obvious prey in my youth.

In high school, I met a guy—let's call him Fun Guy. We crossed paths at a dance club while I was tearing up the dance floor. He couldn't stop complimenting me. I was beautiful, hilarious, the best dancer—on and on.

I remember thinking he acted like he'd been waiting his whole life to meet me. It felt uncomfortable, but I couldn't figure out why.

He was being nothing but flattering—and he was cute.

Soon after we began seeing each other, Fun Guy professed his love. I did not love him, so I didn't say it back. He would drink and manhandle me because I refused to reciprocate. I'd get angry. He'd cry. I'd forgive him.

Until After Prom.

In the middle of the night, he snuck out to the parking lot to have some drinks. When he came back in, he asked me to dance. We stood at the edge of the dance floor, next to tables packed with people taking a break. As soon as I smelled the alcohol on his breath, he launched into another declaration of love.

I rolled my eyes and said nothing.

He was immediately insulted.

He stopped dancing and stared at me, waiting for the words he wanted. I said nothing.

He leveled up to livid. He grabbed my arm, jerked me toward him, and screamed into my face, "SAY IT!"

Still, I said nothing. For the first time, I felt confident standing up to him. He wouldn't dare make a scene in front of all these people. I stared back defiantly.

And then something shifted. My perspective changed—literally. My brain was trying to calculate how I was suddenly airborne.

Before I fully understood what was happening, I landed ass-first on something hard. Drinks went flying. I turned my head and locked eyes with a classmate who now had a lap full of punch. We realized at the same time that Fun Guy had thrown me onto a table full of snacks and drinks.

"Excuse me," I muttered—just as I was being pulled off the table and dragged toward the parking lot.

I had known something was off from the beginning but didn't trust myself. As I matured, I began recognizing that "something's wrong" feeling—a look in someone's eyes, a tone of voice, a shift in energy. Early on, I didn't have the words to describe it, so I kept it to myself.

Unfortunately, Fun Guy wasn't the last time I ignored my instinct.

Years later, I encountered a man—let's call him Nice Man. From the beginning, he made me uncomfortable. He held intense eye contact. He stood too close. He spoke confidently about things he clearly didn't understand. His energy made me anxious.

We interacted over a charity commitment that had a deadline attached. I tried repeatedly for a week to reach him for help. Nothing.

The following week, I stayed after a meeting to address the issue. The energy in the room shifted instantly. His eyes locked onto mine as he stalked toward me, berating me for questioning him. His voice grew loud and angry. His hand was clenched at his side.

Every instinct in me screamed, This is a predator of some kind. People do not move that way.

It was another slap in the face—a reminder.

I darted past him and out to my car. My heart was racing, the hair on my neck standing, my breath tight and shallow.

Months later, I read in the paper that his daughter had filed for a restraining order. I realized whatever that uncomfortable feeling had been, it was trying to guide me—to protect me. I stopped doubting those instinctive reactions. I began to honor them.

Consider this: a rhino is technically a prey animal. They're huge and powerful, with thick skin and massive horns, yet they're easily startled. When something scares them, they use the tools they naturally have to protect themselves. They behave instinctively.

Humans have instinct too—so why don't we use it?

The term "predator" in nature isn't negative. In the wild, ecosystems collapse without them. And just like nature, human personalities serve different roles. A police officer who must seize control in volatile moments? A linebacker who can read the offense instinctively? Those instincts are necessary.

I'm not saying natural "predators" are violent or untrustworthy. I'm saying that in every situation, I try to quiet my mind, observe my instinctual reaction, and trust it. I aim to make instinctual decisions, not fear-based ones.

Both predator and prey are necessary for balance in the wild. Both personality types have strengths that help society function in meaningful ways.

Being a Rhino isn't about being big or tough.

It's about trusting your instincts.

Just when we thought we'd questioned
everything that mattered,
life tapped us on the shoulder and said,
"Actually, there's more."

Sometimes we faced the new challenge head-on.
Sometimes we were sucker-punched and moved
ahead dazed and bruised.

Relax… Seriously. (*Athena*)

If you haven't noticed by now, Hestia and I are kind of like yin and yang. While she was out there learning to set boundaries and protect her empathy, I was the one cannonballing into every new project full speed ahead.

I'm just going to say it—I was a control freak. And honestly? I was proud of it. I had everything organized, color-coded, scheduled, and timed down to the minute: three kids, a demanding career, a husband, a house—you name it, I had it under control.

Eventually, though, I had to stop and ask myself the uncomfortable questions:

Was I always like this?

Why did I become this way?

And did I actually want to stay this way?

I wasn't always like this. I used to be bold and spontaneous—the friend who was always ready to create an adventure. But somewhere along the line, "responsible adult" slowly morphed into "uptight micromanaging lunatic." I convinced myself that being in control made me happy. Spoiler alert: it didn't. It made me stressed, rigid, and exhausting to be around.

How do you go from the fun, risk-taking friend to someone who needs an Excel spreadsheet just to get through the week?

Apparently, one checklist at a time.

And to be fair, I am ambitious. I love big projects. That part of me is useful. But when you focus too hard in one direction, you neglect something else—or someone else. Case in point: the house flip.

We used to joke about flipping a house someday. So naturally, I—control freak that I am—went out and bought one. No plan, no experience, no discussion. Just adrenaline and an overly confident, "I've got this."

On TV, they flip a house in ninety days.

We were weekend warriors doing most of the work ourselves, so I generously gave us six months.

It took two years.

Two long, all-consuming years.

I question the honesty of TV flip timelines.

By the end of the first year, it was obvious we were nowhere close, but we were already in too deep to turn back. Every free moment and every extra dollar went straight into that house. We were constantly covered in dust, exhausted, and juggling one renovation disaster after another.

Somewhere between tearing down walls in that house and building bigger ones inside myself, I had a slap-in-the-face realization: I was no longer controlling my life; my life was controlling me.

I missed the bold, daring version of me. I wanted her back, and I knew I had to find a way to live life again.

So I started practicing letting go—just a little at first. Very little.

And I was terrible at it.

It was almost comical how bad one person could be at not planning. I'd challenge myself to leave an entire weekend open—one whole weekend with no plan at all. I found myself sitting on the couch with my coffee, staring at the wall, asking myself:

"What do people even do when they haven't planned their day?"

I had no idea.

But slowly, I found some balance. I didn't become an unorganized disaster—I still love a good plan—I just stopped loving it at the cost of actually living. I learned to build in flexibility, leave room for joy, and accept that maybe, just maybe, I didn't need to control everything.

There's a quote I love:

"Relax. Nothing is under control."

For the first time, it didn't terrify me. It made sense.

Life already has things figured out.

I just have to show up.

Just when I thought I'd finally mastered relaxing, life smacked me with a reminder that balance isn't optional—especially with your kids—and suddenly I was flat on my back, trying to figure out how I got here.

If this was a slap-you-in-the-face section

Some topics don't land gently. They land with a pause, a laugh that catches, or a quiet "oh."

If that happened here, this page is simply a place to sit with it—no fixing, no figuring it out yet.

If you want to write, write anything. If you don't, that's okay too.

The Wake-Up Call (*Athena*)

The flip was eventually flipped—two years later, not the generous six months I originally declared. But it cost me moments I can't get back. That experience changed me in a way no spreadsheet, checklist, or renovation project ever could.

One of the hardest lessons came from something that had nothing to do with drywall, paint, or renovation disasters. It came from my daughter.

During that two-year flip, our middle child started college. She was responsible and self-motivated, so we didn't check in as closely as we should have. We were knee-deep in renovation chaos every weekend—covered in dust, exhausted, broke, and constantly chasing the next disaster the house threw at us.

She didn't want to bother us.

She didn't want to add to the stress.

So she struggled—quietly.

She didn't tell us she needed us.

She didn't feel like she could.

We didn't find out until her senior year, long after the flip was finished and my marriage was ending. When she finally sat down and told me how alone she'd felt, I was crushed. When she said that she struggled through that first year of college and needed her family, it was like a ton of bricks landed on my chest.

My heart broke.

And as I fought back tears, one question echoed in my mind:

How did I let this happen?

She had been struggling in silence.

I had been too distracted to see it.

Did she try to reach out?

Thinking back, I remember she did ask if we could come visit a couple of times. I remember my answer too: "We are going to be at the flip house—why don't you come here this weekend?" With her class schedule and two or three jobs, she couldn't.

How did I not see that it was more than an idea?

Did other people see this?

I'm her mother. I should have known. I should have seen it. The disappointment in myself was overwhelming, and in that moment, I would have given anything to go back and do things differently—just to spare her the pain I had caused.

She needed me, and I wasn't there.

That was my most important job as a mother: to be there when she needed me—and I wasn't.

It was a painful slap in the face—the kind that forces you to stop and question everything.

My way of doing things wasn't just imperfect—it was hurting the people I loved.

And that moment taught me something I wish I'd learned sooner:

Strong kids need checking on too—sometimes more than anyone.

I learned that the hard way because I grew up being the strong one myself. And when she spoke, I recognized that same quiet strength in her—the "I'm fine" mask, the independence, the instinct to hold everything together without asking for help. It was like watching a younger version of myself struggle in the exact same way I used to.

That realization was hard to swallow.

Not because she blamed me—but because I saw myself reflected in her hurt.

And that's when the wake-up call really landed:

Strength without support isn't strength at all.

It's isolation dressed up as independence.

That moment shifted everything. It changed the way I saw myself, my relationships, and the walls I had built. It pushed me to find a way back to the present, balanced, connected version of myself—not just for me, but for the people I loved most.

I had to step back and take an honest look at who I had become and how I'd chosen to approach life. I'd always taken pride in being able to handle it all… but was that really the goal? Was everything just a checklist to power through?

I learned—in a very painful way—that I needed a different kind of strength. Not the kind that simply got me through the hard moments, but the kind I could rely on to actually take me where I wanted to go.

Weight Training (*Athena*)

After that wake-up call, I realized it was time for me to hit the gym—but not the one with treadmills and weight benches. I had been building all the wrong muscles, and my training routine needed some major adjusting.

This is probably an unpopular opinion, but the label "strong woman" always felt like nails on a chalkboard to me. All my adult life, I heard things like, "You're such a strong woman," and "I'm so proud of how strong you are." And I know people meant it as a compliment.

But here's the truth: I wasn't strong for the reasons people thought. I was strong because I knew how to build strong walls to protect myself. And the really strange part is that I knew exactly how to let people in just enough—to have friends and surface-level family relationships—but never far enough to see the real me. I picture it like a foyer or entry hallway—the part of your house you keep clean enough for someone to take a couple of steps in, but that's it. That's as far as you go, because I don't want you to see the rest. That was as far as most people were allowed to go.

It wasn't until I finally started removing some of those bricks that I saw things differently. I may have looked strong from the outside, but true strength—the kind that actually shapes a life—looks nothing like what I had been praised for.

Tearing down what I'd spent decades constructing took a level of strength I didn't know I had. Keeping people out was easy. Letting people in? Letting someone new see the real me? That was terrifying.

So when I finally decided to let someone new in, I had no idea how to do it. I remember telling Hestia, "I think I'm falling in love with this guy," and she said, "That's great, I'm happy for you." I stared at her like she'd grown a second head.

"That is not great."

She blinked, confused. "How is falling in love not great?"

"It scares the shit out of me! That is far from great."

And honestly, that was probably the first time Hestia ever saw me hit the brakes instead of charging ahead. It was a big deal for both of us.

If I was going to embrace this whole "falling in love" thing, I was going to have to let someone see the real me. And I had never done that before. Not really.

I always knew the real version of me was buried back there, but she'd been hurt so much. If I let her out from behind those walls, was she strong enough—truly strong enough—to withstand whatever happened next?

This was going to take the kind of strength I had never practiced. After a divorce and a full identity overhaul, did I actually have what it took? What if I got hurt again? What if I failed? What if I tried so hard and still ended up alone? Would that be worse than not trying at all?

I could have chosen someone easier—someone who didn't make me feel the need to grow. But that's what I'd had before, and I already knew I didn't want that anymore. If I wanted something real, I had to become the strong woman everyone thought I already was.

So I let myself fall in love. And let me tell you—if I ever wrote a love story based on my actual experience of "falling in love," it would be pure torture for the reader. It wasn't rainbows and roses. It was hard, uncomfortable work—the kind that forces you to confront everything you've avoided.

I wanted to give up so many times. I did give up at one point. You'll hear that part of the story later, and somehow, I found the strength to try again.

There were plenty of times when I got in my own way—I mean, I was so conflicted that I would literally do things some people would probably refer to as self-sabotage.

It took years to work through each layer of those bricks and sort through everything underneath. And the truth is, that kind of work puts real pressure on a relationship. Most relationships wouldn't have survived what we went through. We both walked through hell while I tried to untangle everything. But even if our relationship hadn't made it, I knew I had to keep doing the work. I needed to know what I was really made of, and it took so much determination and grit to do that—but I needed to do it, for me.

Because that's what real weight training is: learning to carry what's yours, set down what isn't, and keep showing up even when the reps feel impossible.

And this version of me—I am proud to own.

I am a strong woman.

Alright, you got me—there was so much more to tackle.

And once we started working through it, it became impossible to ignore how all of it had shaped us—and what we needed to do about it.

It turns out we all carry some kind of bags—different shapes, different sizes, different weights. And some of them we've been hauling around for so long, we don't even notice the strain anymore.

Bags
(Hestia)

When I was in my teens and early twenties, I carried cute little trendy bags. I loved having a bag that matched my outfit—and of course, my shoes.

After my second child came along, I eventually switched to throwing my wallet into the diaper bag. Carrying my purse, the baby's diaper bag, my oldest's sippy cup, the baby, and wrangling my toddler was beyond exhausting.

After having three kids and moving past the diaper-bag phase, I found that my purse was never big enough. Whenever the family went out, my purse would get heavier and heavier throughout the day. At the end of the night, when inventorying my purse, it was not at all uncommon to find my husband's wallet, my daughter's earrings, my oldest son's cell phone, and my youngest son's uneaten snack. That was in addition to all the extra "just in case" items

I'd thrown in—a small package of baby wipes, granola bars, gum, and a bottle of water.

As moms, I think we accept responsibility for the baggage of others. I believe moms are hardwired that way. By the end of the day, I would be tired, grumpy, and confused about when all this baggage was added to my load.

Honestly, I eventually just leaned into it and started carrying a backpack.

At some point, we all arrive at the same situation with our emotional baggage. We settle in to carry it because we're used to it. We just try to keep it from spilling out at dinner.

When I was in elementary school, I was repeatedly sexually abused by a distant relative. I was obviously too young to understand that the abuse was actually about control. He enjoyed the emotions that surfaced every time he was around. Each time I encountered him, the emotions I felt during the abuse resurfaced as though I were right back in the very same situation—feeling all the fear, shame, and anger. My skin would crawl. I would feel nausea, burning anxiety in my chest, uncontrollable trembling, humiliation, and hatred—for him and for myself.

I couldn't process my trauma because I was still living it.

After some time, I became better at hiding the emotions he enjoyed seeing. I only let myself show hatred and anger. I was certain there was not another soul in the world who would understand me. I believed that anyone who knew my secret would be disgusted with me—just as I was with myself.

In the years that followed, I had several unhealthy romantic relationships.

Eventually, there was a guy—no one special, just a guy. His friend dated my friend, so we ended up spending some time together. We dated briefly, and I broke it off with him to date someone else. He seemed to take it okay.

He still came around because his friend still dated mine. One night, I was down about the newest guy and decided to spend the evening drinking away my sorrows. When I started drinking, there were several people with me, including Mr. No One Special. Eventually, I was slapped in the face by the realization that it was only the two of us—and I had had more to drink than I intended.

My intention was to go to my room and leave him alone in the living room. I tried to stand, but my legs didn't cooperate. I couldn't walk. I tried to crawl, but I could barely control my legs.

He rose from the couch and stalked toward me. Even in my drunken state, a familiar feeling began to register in my head...

I felt a burning stab in my chest. My heart began pounding. The hair on the back of my neck stood on end. I suddenly couldn't catch my breath.

That familiar feeling was terror.

No. No. No.

By then, he—like me—realized that I was too intoxicated to walk, or crawl, or resist. It was too late for me to stop what I now realized was going to happen.

The following day, my roommate and close friend took one look at me and knew something was very wrong. She was kind, caring, patient, and supportive. I began describing the circumstances of the previous night. I couldn't get through the story, but she got the gist. She simply sat with me and cried.

She very likely saved me.

At that moment, I did not believe I could carry this agony any longer—nor did I want to.

Had she left me alone, I probably wouldn't be here now. I treasure her friendship to this day.

Obviously, I was left, again, with crippling baggage. At first, it was simply too overwhelming to deal with. I couldn't even say the words. I did the only thing I knew to do: drink. I drank often, and I drank a lot, in an attempt to numb myself to feelings I did not want to feel.

In reality, I was becoming an emotional volcano. Every so often, I would erupt into a bout of overwhelming depression. When I did, my roommate sat quietly and let me cry—but she was there.

When I met my husband, I knew early on that I loved him. I could not bring myself to be vulnerable with him, despite knowing I loved him. Eventually, I felt so much like a fraud that I spilled my guts about all the abuse. I felt dirty and inadequate. I couldn't look him in the eyes once he had heard my secrets.

To my surprise, he stayed. He even admired the strength it took for me to bear the weight of this burden. He didn't blame me at all. It was because of his acceptance and respect that I began to look at the situation rationally—and without guilt.

I struggle with control issues. I know that, in reality, control is an illusion. This world throws things at us on a daily basis that we could never anticipate. As hard as I tried, I could never really feel as if I had achieved control over my life. The truth is, I never will. I have to be flexible and accept what happens to me. I can only control how I react to life.

My toughest struggle has been with forgiveness. I carried a fear with me every day that I was too terrified to admit to myself—the fear of seeing any of the men who abused me. Just the sight of them would threaten to undo all the walls I had built to protect myself and all the denial that helped me get through each day.

I had no intention of forgiving them. They did not deserve my forgiveness.

They deserved to have their genitals filleted and served to them on a flaming spike.

Ultimately, I was able to separate what they deserved from what I deserved. By letting go of the hurt and fear, allowing myself to work through feelings I feared would break me, and shifting my focus from my past to my future, I found peace.

I have decided that I am no longer willing to carry their bags. I choose to seek out peace for myself.

Oh—and of course, a fabulous bag that holds only what I want and is unapologetically a reflection of me. Picture a brilliant pink-and-black Kate Spade that perfectly matches my brilliant pink Adidas sneakers.

That's My Bag! (Unfortunately) (Athena)

Throughout this book, I've mentioned baggage—the stuff we carry from old hurts and old versions of ourselves. By this point, I had already identified plenty of mine. But knowing you have baggage and actually learning how to put it down are two very different things.

For most of my life, I thought other people were the ones flaunting their baggage. You know the type—the ones who are always telling you how they were wronged today, who drag drama into every room. I worked hard to dodge their chaos, only to realize I'd been walking right beside them, juggling an entire full set of my own baggage—from the small cosmetic case I could grab easily all the way to a huge suitcase that was over the weight limit, and everything in between.

In my relationships, I held onto that one thing someone did that hurt me because I thought it would protect me. I brought it up in arguments, and I used it to justify my reactions. I clung to it like a security blanket. And in a way, it did exactly what I wanted—it put space between me and the person who hurt me.

It's crazy how I can reach into my baggage and pull out exact memories from years ago, yet struggle to remember what I had for lunch yesterday. I can literally recall something someone said to me in high school that upset me.

I didn't fully understand how my baggage was affecting my relationships until I started noticing what it was costing me. That "safe distance" doesn't just block the negative—it blocks the positive too. It was nearly impossible to grow or nurture a relationship when my hands were full of baggage.

I started noticing this in several of my relationships as I tried to reclaim a more free-spirited version of myself. I wanted healthier connections with friends and family—but some of those relationships came with history. Hurt. Things I'd never fully dealt with.

The first step was admitting I didn't want those things standing in the way anymore. And while I can write that in a quick, easy sentence, that is not the way it happened.

It wasn't one decision or a single moment of clarity. It was choosing—again and again—to value the people in my life more than the hurt I'd been carrying for years. Letting go didn't happen all at once. It happened in pieces.

With my new goals, I had to start somewhere.

I told myself I'd clear the air. Let go of old hurts. Lower some of the walls I had built.

"Talk to them," I thought. "Tell them how it made you feel. If they value the relationship, they'll be open to that… right? That sounds like a good place to start. They will be open to that."

Well… not exactly.

If open conversations aren't something you—or they—are used to, it takes practice. My first attempts did not go well.

Hestia had a front-row seat to this era, and at one point she told me, "You have a punch-them-in-the-gut approach." She wasn't wrong. I can be blunt—brutally honest, even—so my early attempts led to defensive, messy conversations. I had to come back later with a different approach before any real progress was made.

I remember one specific attempt where I decided to take a piece of my baggage to someone and sort through it. There were two metaphorical slaps in the face during that conversation, and I was equally blindsided by both.

I told myself I'd just say it—get it out. No beating around the bush. I delivered it bluntly, with zero finesse or emotion. I thought I was "speaking my truth." In reality, I was punching the other person in the gut.

When I learned my sister had taken my ex-husband's side in a disagreement, I was hurt. So I confronted her with, "You really hurt me when you took his side, and we need to figure this out because that is not OK."

I was so wrapped up in my own hurt that I hadn't even considered her side before throwing that first emotional punch. What I expected to be a beautiful kumbaya moment of clearing the air turned into a rude awakening.

She had valid issues of her own—and I wasn't ready for that.

I had actually hurt her through my actions. In a conversation with someone else about my impending divorce, I made a comment. Without knowing it, I had stumbled upon one of her triggers, and the person I was talking to shared my comment with her. It was incredibly hurtful to her, and from her point of view, I could see why she sided with him.

When I stored something away for years, I isolated only my side of the issue. I preserved my memory of it—but not theirs. Old, smelly baggage is rarely stored with love or empathy. So when I pulled out this poorly packed memory, I was shocked to learn there was much more to the story than I'd ever realized. I hadn't been so unjustly treated after all—I was part of the issue too.

That was slap number two.

I learned that when I pull out an old piece of baggage, it's wise to sort through it privately first—with love, empathy, and honesty—before dumping it on someone else.

Empathy is not my natural gift, but I tried. I found another old piece of baggage and thought, "Okay, here's my chance to look at this from the other person's perspective and approach it better."

I sucked at it.

I came up with a few logical explanations for how things might have looked from their side. I fully expected to hear some version of that in the conversation.

This time, I opened with a question instead of an accusation, giving them the opportunity to tell their side. I fully expected they would apologize and we could hug and move on.

Instead, their perspective was so wildly different that I remember thinking:

Were we even talking about the same situation?

But they didn't feel punched in the gut this time. And you have to take the small wins.

Working through this stuff sometimes feels like trudging through a swamp in sweatpants—so stop and appreciate how far you've come.

The next time I approached one of those difficult conversations, I leaned less on logic and more on empathy. I got closer. And a few tries later… I actually got it right.

That was a huge win. I was genuinely proud of that one.

I also learned that grace has to go both ways. If the person you're talking to isn't used to emotional conversations, they might react defensively, shut down, or freeze. I had to remind myself to give patience where I wanted patience—and to allow space where things felt uncomfortable. Building new ways of communicating takes time. On both sides.

If this was a slap-you-in-the-face section

Some topics don't land gently. They land with a pause, a laugh that catches, or a quiet "oh."

If that happened here, this page is simply a place to sit with it—no fixing, no figuring it out yet.

If you want to write, write anything. If you don't, that's okay too.

Learning to live without hauling your past around is no easy task.

It isn't something you can just drop and walk away from.

But small choices—made consistently—begin to create a more balanced life.

And one powerful step is learning to live in the moment.

Live In The Moment

(Athena & Hestia)

Hestia

"Live in the moment."

It might be one of the most insightful statements ever uttered—and one of the hardest for humans to actually understand.

Cesar Millan once said, "In nature, a dog's life is very simple... Dogs live moment by moment. They do not worry about the future or dwell on the past."

I've thought about that quote often.

My first real experience with taking stock of everything I had survived came early in my relationship with my husband. We weren't married yet, but I already knew I loved him—and he told me he loved me too. My shame, however, was so deep that I felt like a fraud. I truly didn't believe I deserved his love.

One night, we were at my place watching a movie. He held me close, snuggled on the couch—my back leaning against his chest, his arms wrapped around me. He hugged me tightly and whispered that he loved me.

"Me too," I said.

He was quiet for a moment, then gently asked, "Are you sure?"

I turned to look at him, confused. He continued, "You don't sound confident when you say that."

My eyes burned. I fought back tears.

"Do you have secrets?" I asked.

"Everyone has secrets," he said cautiously.

"No—secrets that hurt like your guts are twisting?"

He told me I could tell him—that he loved me and that it wouldn't change.

"You haven't heard it yet," I whispered. "I love you... and I don't want to go further until you know. Because if you're going to bail..."

He sat up straighter and waited quietly. I turned toward the TV.

"Please don't look at me when I say this."

He nodded and looked forward too.

And then I told him everything.

I told him about what happened in kindergarten. I told him about the repeated abuse from ages nine to twelve. I told him about Mr. No One Special. I spilled every secret I had carried alone for years. By the time I stopped talking, we were both crying. I still couldn't look at him.

"I can't believe you survived all that," he finally said.

I turned toward him, confused.

Tears streamed down his face. "I am so sorry that all of that happened to you."

I sat in stunned silence. Not only did he not run away—he told me I was strong. He told me the shame, guilt, and humiliation were not mine. They belonged to the men who hurt me.

That moment shifted something inside me. If I hadn't found the courage to speak my truth in that moment, I may not have the relationship with my soulmate that I cherish today.

My past abuse left scars. To move beyond the pain, I had to accept that these things were done to me—I did nothing to deserve them.

I no longer accept shame, guilt, or responsibility for the actions of others. Acknowledging my wounds taught me that I have the courage to let others know I am wounded. The things that caused me crippling pain also revealed a strength I didn't know I had. I refused to submit to my abusers then, and I will not start now.

Today, I strive to be the person I want to be. When I fall short, I forgive myself and begin again tomorrow.

When I need inspiration, I watch *The Dog Whisperer*. A dog is a masterclass in living in the moment. They judge us by our energy. They process instinctually. I can scold my dog for knocking over the trash can, and two minutes later she's following me around the kitchen, smiling, hoping I drop a crumb. No grudges. Just love. Her love is her guiding light, and she doesn't let past scoldings dim it.

Living in the moment, for me, means focusing on what's happening now—not replaying the past. We're all the sum of our experiences, and mine left marks on my soul. But here's my perspective:

I get to decide how those marks shape me.

If I never pause to reflect on what each experience taught me, then change happens *to* me instead of *through* me.

When I choose to learn from each moment, I decide what to carry forward and what to leave behind. That's how I move ahead lighter, wiser, and stronger.

Eventually, after the whole Nice Man situation, I told Athena and our third bestie about my experiences. That conversation led me to share more of my earlier abuse. The more I talk about it, the less power it has over me. I choose not to feel destroyed by it—I will be empowered.

Unlike me, Athena didn't realize she was holding onto her own baggage at all. She believed she had rationalized hers away.

Athena

One of the biggest reasons I struggled to "live in the moment" was because half the time... I wasn't actually in it. I thought I was—but really, I was reacting to old hurts that had nothing to do with the moment in front of me.

My buried baggage seeped into everything like emotional dye in the wash. Suddenly, every interaction was tinted a color it wasn't supposed to be.

A harmless comment felt like criticism.
A simple question felt like judgment.
A pause—the worst of all—felt like rejection.

I wasn't responding to the person in front of me.
I was responding to every unprocessed moment I had never dealt with.

And honestly? I still struggle with this, especially in emotionally charged conversations—most often with my husband. Those conversations usually go like this:

Him: "That's not what I said."

Me: "Yes it is. It's exactly what you said."

Him: "What were my exact words?"

(He's learned this trick. I don't know if he knows why it works, but he knows it does.)

Sometimes I repeat his words correctly… and other times I've rewritten them into something completely unrecognizable.

That's usually my clue that I've left the actual moment and wandered into the emotional storage closet—the one where I keep old hurts, outdated fears, and a few pieces of baggage I swear I threw away years ago.

When that happens, I have to pause and remind myself:

"This reaction belongs to the past. Not the present."

And that tiny moment of awareness—noticing the shift—is the first step toward actually living in the moment, instead of reliving an old one.

Learning to stay in the moment was the first big step toward finally being able to live in it.

Your Turn

What idea from these topics stayed with you longer than the others?

If you want to write:

What felt familiar?

What felt uncomfortable?

Now that we acknowledge that we should let go of our baggage, how do we actually accomplish that?
Easier said than done.

And no one tells you that you're going to have to try multiple times to put that baggage down.
That's a real kick in the khakis!

Are We There Yet?

(Athena)

Wow. I had uncovered some crazy shit. And facing it was brutal. But at the time, I was completely convinced the hardest part was over.

In classic "Control Freak Me" fashion, I thought the rest would be easy. In my head, it went something like this:

Okay, great. I found all the broken pieces. Now all I have to do is put them back together exactly how I want them. No problem. Give me a plan, a timeline, a checklist, and I'll be emotionally restored by the end of the day.

I genuinely believed emotional healing was something I could handle with focus and efficiency.

Instead of a simple: dig a hole → fix the issue → fill the hole, it became: dig a hole → immediately hit a new issue → get emotionally bulldozed → stop → stare at a wall for ten minutes → then try to figure out what tool I'm supposed to use for this new mess.

Very quickly, I realized I had no idea what tools I was missing, how many I needed, or where the hell to get them.

Up until then, my emotional toolkit consisted of crying, talking, journaling, and overthinking—basically a Fisher-Price *My First Feelings* kit. Those tools were fine for surface-level stuff, but not for the deeper layers I was suddenly tripping over.

I needed more.

Then, during a conversation with a friend, she mentioned she had tried something called Reiki. She admitted she didn't fully understand it, but she said it helped her uncover emotional blockages she didn't know she had.

I was intrigued.

I've always had a slight nature-energy side—the part of me that's just a little hippy-dippy—but I had never explored that part of myself on a deeper level. This was the first time I'd seriously considered leaning into it. So, in a curious-but-skeptical moment, I booked my own appointment immediately.

That session was the first time I learned we have energy centers—chakras—where emotional experiences can get stuck. When emotions aren't processed, they create blockages that influence everything: your reactions, your fears, your choices, your relationships.

I had lived over forty years in this body and knew none of this.

As we worked, I discovered many of my issues were rooted in childhood and family relationships. Trying to make logical sense of it didn't work (shocking, I know). Healing wasn't linear or neat. Everything was connected—like a pile of cords that somehow knot themselves when no one touches them.

I had to stop trying to solve everything like a math problem and start letting the process unfold.

So I started at the beginning—the beginning-beginning—before I ever took my first breath.

I had always known the basic version of my origin story:

My parents were casually involved. My mother became pregnant. She told my father. He instantly checked out—permanently. He lived fifteen miles away and never once tried to see me, ask about me, or even acknowledge I existed. I had convinced myself at a young age that I was better off without someone like him in my life.

But when I looked at it with new awareness, without the protective logic I'd used for decades, it hit differently.

I wasn't just better off without him.

I was abandoned.

And that wound had shaped my life more than I ever allowed myself to admit. Those were bricks I had been handed before I was even born—bricks I later used to build the biggest, strongest walls imaginable.

Reiki didn't magically fix anything, but it gave me direction, language, and a sense of where the blockages were hiding. And it helped me discover something I didn't know I had:

A freaking emotional bulldozer.

The same force I used to build my walls?

I could use it to tear them down.

As I kept working through these layers, I realized I needed stronger tools than crying and journaling. One of the most powerful tools I found was the letter-burning exercise.

I wrote a brutally honest letter to my father—not the polite, logical version of me, but the uncensored emotional version. The one who was furious, hurt, abandoned, and finally ready to admit it. I wrote pages of truth I had never allowed myself to feel.

I started calmly, writing about the things he missed in my life and telling him I was probably better off without him. But by the end of the second page, I really let him have it. My hands shaking with anger, I called him a piece of shit for abandoning me and a horrible excuse of a man for not even acknowledging my existence. Tears streamed down my cheeks as I wrote that I truly hated him.

After releasing emotions I had held for a lifetime—and several pages later—I stepped away. A few days later, I reread the letter, added a few more things, and when it was finally complete, I burned it.

I swear I felt the anger leave my body.

When that paper turned to ash, I felt like I could finally start healing the scars underneath those emotions. I wasn't ready to forgive him—that took years—but the anger was gone.

It shocked me how much I had been carrying without even realizing it.

The walls I built out of childhood anger protected me once, but now they were preventing me from experiencing the depth of love I wanted. And that's when I knew:

It was finally time to start tearing those walls down.

And just when I thought I had finally gotten somewhere…

I realized I was only at the beginning.

Ugh to the Ughs, Growth is Hard!

(Athena)

During a conversation with a friend not long ago, I said, "I swear, I have to learn everything the hard way."

He didn't even lift his head before responding, "That's because you're stubborn."

As much as I hate to admit it, he was right.

Growth has always been hard for me—not because I didn't want to grow, but because I had no idea how much of myself I had buried, ignored, or mislabeled over the years.

When I finally began doing the real work after my divorce, it felt like I shattered into a hundred pieces. Each piece represented a belief, a reaction, a coping mechanism, a fear, a habit—and suddenly I had to pick up each one and ask myself what to do with it.

Do I keep this part of me?

Do I reshape it?

Or is this one of the pieces I finally need to let go?

Some pieces surprised me in a good way. Others were just dusty and needed attention. And some revealed things I had avoided my entire adult life. What made this process so overwhelming was realizing how much of who I thought I was had been shaped unintentionally—by childhood experiences, survival patterns, and unspoken beliefs I never questioned. It was disorienting to see how many of my reactions had nothing to do with the present and everything to do with the past.

Then came the day when two different friends—in two separate conversations—told me the same thing:

"You struggle with certain things because you have a low level of empathy."

I wasn't offended. I was stunned—mostly because once they said it, I instantly saw exactly what they meant. They each gave me examples, and although it was painful to hear, I couldn't deny any of it. When two people who don't talk to each other tell you the same thing on the same day, it's probably time to pay attention.

That was the moment I went searching for something—anything—to help me understand what I had clearly been missing. That search led me to *The Art of Empathy* by Karla McLaren, and that book opened a door I didn't even know existed. It helped me understand emotions—not just other people's, but my own—in a way I had never explored.

Looking back, I understand why empathy had never been my strong suit. I grew up relying on logic, not emotion. Logic made sense. Logic was clean, reliable, predictable. I used to say, "It doesn't matter how I feel; this is the logical choice." And I believed that was maturity.

It wasn't.

That approach works beautifully with spreadsheets and scheduling.
It works terribly with humans.

One of the clearest examples happened when I ran a daycare. My husband's step-sister needed part-time care for her baby. Because she had family support, she only needed a few days a week. But financially, for me, that spot needed to be full-time.

So I sat her down—calmly, rationally—and laid out her options. To me, it was fair, reasonable, and clearly explained.

She cried.

Family members got involved.

Suddenly, I was the villain in a story I didn't understand.

Somehow—literally, before I knew what hit me—I was swept up in a whole bunch of family drama.

What the heck just happened?

I felt like I had been hit over the head with a shovel and dumped in the trunk of a car, with no idea how I got there or where this was going.

I felt confused and angry. She was being emotional about a logical issue, which I thought was weak and dramatic—and obviously wrong—while I was anchored in logic, which was obviously right.

I honestly thought they were all crazy. What are you getting so upset about?

What I didn't see was the emotional side at all.

To her, this wasn't a business decision—it was her child, her stability, her trust in me. It felt like I had ripped away her sense of security. To a mother, having someone you trust to care for your child while you work is priceless, and I treated it like a math problem.

That moment was one of the first times I realized how often I responded without any awareness of someone else's emotional experience—not out of coldness, but out of habit, out of survival, out of a set of patterns I didn't even know I was following.

As I kept picking up those shattered pieces of myself, I started noticing the same pattern show up again and again.

I lived most of my life from the neck up—analyzing, planning, rationalizing. Feeling was optional. Usually skipped.

And because of that, I missed things.
I misunderstood people.
I hurt them without meaning to.
I shut them out without realizing that's what I was doing.

Learning to change that has been a difficult undertaking. It requires slowing down, noticing my reactions, questioning where they come from, and being willing to sit with emotions I used to bulldoze right past. It means considering how something might feel to the other person—not just whether it makes sense on paper.

I'm learning. Slowly. Imperfectly. Sometimes clumsily.

Sometimes with the emotional grace of a toddler trying to walk while holding a cherry pie.

But I can feel the difference.

I notice when I react instead of respond.
I notice when I want to shut down.
I notice when something feels uncomfortable—and I stay anyway.

There are still plenty of "ugh" moments. Probably always will be.

But now, when they show up, I don't see them as proof that something's wrong.
I see them as part of the work.

And for the first time, that feels like growth I can actually live with.

Family Heirlooms (Athena)

Sometimes we end up with things we don't love. Sometimes we call them family heirlooms, but let's be honest—they aren't always treasures. Yet we hold onto them simply because they were passed down from previous generations.

I've often laughed to myself wondering whether the person who first brought that object into the family even liked it. I imagine them staring at it every day, swearing they'd replace it as soon as they could—and then somehow it ends up being handed down for decades, each family disliking it as much as the last.

I had a quilt like that. It felt like every scrap of ugly fabric was saved until there was finally enough to make a quilt. None of the pieces matched. There were several dull brown squares next to bright blue and red flowers, surrounded by pink and lavender blocks. There seemed to be no plan—just chaos stitched together. It never made me feel warm or cozy. Isn't that the whole point of a quilt?

One day, I decided I was done. I wrestled with guilt for a while, but eventually dropped that quilt off at a donation center and never looked back. I no longer had to walk into my bedroom every day and wish it wasn't there.

As I began working through my emotional baggage, I realized I had "family heirlooms" of my own—and some of them were the emotional equivalent of that ugly quilt I'd been living with but not loving.

I've shared about the nonexistent relationship with my dad and how I had to process all that locked-away anger. But eventually, I had to face my relationship with my mother too. This one surprised me.

Once I started digging, I found so many conflicting emotions. Working through them required everything I had learned up to that point and every tool in my emotional toolbelt. I had to dig deep for this one.

It's complicated being raised by a single parent. They're in roles they aren't always equipped for. While I admired the effort my mom made to be everything she could for my sister and me, I also felt resentment. This wasn't the sharp, fiery anger I carried for my father. This was a tangled mess—positive and negative twisted together—the perfect recipe for an unhealthy, sometimes toxic relationship.

My mother has been described as the "Ric Flair of grandmas," and honestly, that's accurate. She doesn't hide her joy. She can lift the vibration in a room within seconds. Her laugh carries for miles, and you will absolutely hear a whoop when her favorite song comes on. I am proud to say I inherited much of that from her. She is loyal, kind, giving, caring, and deeply empathetic—the last of which I most definitely did not inherit. These parts of her shaped me, and I'm grateful for them.

But the things she wasn't able to give also shaped me—and those were the heirlooms I had to work through. Finding a starting point was hard. Some days, all I could see were the ugly brown patches on the quilt. There were moments of anger, disappointment, resentment…and hurt. There, I said it. I had a lot of hurt from my mom.

Once I accepted that this was another quilt I needed to deal with, I needed tools—and honestly, I wasn't sure I had the right ones. Thank goodness I had a counselor who understood me, because I needed both humor and strong guidance, both of which she was great at. But surprisingly, one of the most effective tools for this job turned out to be empathy. Luckily, I had already begun working on that skill, because it took every ounce I could find. And since I was still new at empathy, it was awkward and clumsy.

I was angry with my mother for being a single parent. Not having a father created a lack of security in more ways than I realized. There were times when we had no food, and times I felt unprotected without a man in the house. I didn't get the fatherly guidance I needed. So yes—I had classic "daddy issues."

Because of her experiences with men, one of the "heirlooms" I received from my mom and the women in my family was a very clear message:

You cannot trust men.

I don't remember the first time I heard it or how often it was actually said, but I do remember being at a family event and observing the banter filled with these undertones. These were not just jokes about men—they were beliefs.

That message became a massive pile of bricks I used to build my reinforced walls—bricks I'm still dismantling today so I can have strong, loving relationships with the men in my life. And this didn't just affect romantic relationships; it affected every male relationship I had.

Once I realized this particular heirloom wasn't mine to carry, I opened my notebook and dug out my letter-writing tool. I wrote her a letter explaining how her decisions had impacted me and that I was giving the ownership back to her—releasing myself from the weight of it. The letter was different from the one I wrote to my dad, but just as effective. I burned it when I was done and let that blockage fall away. I can't say our relationship changed much at that point, but I was finally open to trying—and willing to put effort into healing.

Even though I released the feelings, the trust issues themselves took years to dismantle. That was a quilt I carried much longer.

And because I still had a relationship with my mom, I knew I needed to work toward forgiving her sooner. So I tried out my newly developing skill of empathy. I asked her more about her childhood—which was tragic. I had known some of it, but only the child version. As an adult, I was given the adult version, or at least most of it. As I listened, I began to understand her more. I saw the pain she had carried her whole life, and my heart broke for her.

Through those conversations—and a lot of meditation—I was finally able to use empathy to begin forgiving her. Seeing her experience more clearly didn't erase my disappointments, but it softened them. Understanding how my childhood impacted me—and how complicated untangling it all had been—gave me empathy for how her childhood shaped the decisions she made. And how could I fault her for that?

I had done the exact same thing.

That realization hit hard. It wasn't easy to face. But it was true:

We all do the best we can with the tools we have at the time.

So even though I wasn't good at using my new tool, the first step was simply to try. I made mistakes. I had to redo some of it. But I made progress—and I began dismantling that ugly quilt one square at a time.

If this was a slap-you-in-the-face section

Some topics don't land gently. They land with a pause, a laugh that catches, or a quiet "oh."

If that happened here, this page is simply a place to sit with it—no fixing, no figuring it out yet.

If you want to write, write anything. If you don't, that's okay too.

Letting go of the heavy stuff we've carried is a huge undertaking. It's a tremendous task.

Equally important is learning to protect your boundaries. If you don't, life will pile more onto your shoulders than you ever intended to carry.

No one needs that. Get to know your inner bitch.

Inner Bitch

(Hestia)

Let's be real — we all have an inner bitch. And I personally do not understand why anyone would be disappointed by that. The Bitch is my superhero.

Now, I know some people have a tougher time recognizing when to unleash her. And some of us use her more sparingly than others. But when used properly, the Bitch can circumvent catastrophic situations.

Don't believe she's necessary? Observe...

My son was required to read a book and take a test over its contents. The book was very long and a bit of a complicated read. I assume that, for these reasons, the teacher did not believe he had read the book. Just to be clear, there was no valid reason for this doubt.

This teacher proceeded to call me — during class — to question my son's honesty, stating that the book was long and not easy.

Um... excuse me?

I unleash the Bitch.

Teacher: "I am inquiring about the score your son received on the test. He received a 90%."

The Bitch: "So, you called to insult me by insinuating that my son cheated and I allowed it?"

Teacher: "I assure you the purpose of this call is simply to verify his claim to have read the book."

The Bitch: "What did the other parents say when they received calls to verify their children had read the book?"

There is a pregnant pause on the line. The teacher explains that I am the only parent she called.

At this point, the Bitch goes from assertive to aggressive.

The Bitch: "You will either telephone all the other parents or apologize to my child for attempting to humiliate him in front of his class. If neither of these things happen, I will see you in the Superintendent's office tomorrow. I had better hear the amazing story of how you apologized tonight when he gets home. Now run along and handle your shit."

Click.

The Bitch defends our boundaries when dipshits attempt to bulldoze them. Boundaries are necessary in every relationship, and every single one of us will find ourselves in situations where those boundaries are tested.

Sometimes they're tested by people in positions of authority. Some situations require the Bitch to be assertive; others require her to be aggressive. And the difference between assertive and aggressive?

Finesse.

I once had a boss who was an "ends justify the means" type of person. One day, he came into my office with a request. He asked me to review reports from another department — reports I had no reason to see under normal circumstances.

What he actually wanted was for me to dig through them for any possible discrepancy so he could use that information as leverage over the department head. I was extremely uncomfortable — not only with the request itself, but with the fact that he asked me in person so there would be no paper trail.

If that department discovered what I was doing, I would be in a tough spot.

I needed the Bitch to mull it over.

The next morning, I emailed him asking for specifics: which reports, what issues he wanted me to look for, and what the intended purpose was — all framed professionally, as if I were eager to help.

He immediately replied that I must have misunderstood his request and that he'd be happy to give it a look himself.

The Bitch once again defended my boundaries with beautiful efficiency.

I wholeheartedly believe the Inner Bitch is necessary. She is the part of me that identifies attempts to take advantage of me or bulldoze my boundaries. She seeks to protect me — and the people I love. She is my righteous indignation.

Sometimes when my Bitch-senses tingle, I have a moment to pause and evaluate her concerns. If possible, I take time to decide whether assertiveness or aggression is appropriate. Other times, I have to let the Bitch take the lead in the moment.

Regardless, I trust my Inner Bitch — and I act accordingly.

Your Turn

What idea from these topics stayed with you longer than the others?

If you want to write:

What felt familiar?

What felt uncomfortable?

Understanding when we are defending our boundaries is crucial. We must never use the bitch willy-nilly.

When hurt happens, understanding the difference between boundary pushing and someone stumbling upon a trauma trigger is key.

The Nasty Four-Letter Word

(Athena)

In the English language, there's one word that used to send me running in the opposite direction. One four-letter word that made me cringe just thinking about it:

HURT.

Hurt was something I was taught could not be tolerated. It was the ultimate betrayal and meant the relationship had to end.

Extreme?

Yes. But that belief was reinforced my whole life—partly learned from my family and partly from my own experiences. I saw it play out so many times, but I never actually heard anyone say, *You hurt me.*

I heard, *You pissed me off,* or *Who does she think she is?* Even, *I am never talking to them again*—but never, *That hurt.*

Even now, it might sound like I went through twenty-three years of marriage without ever being hurt—which would be impossible—but the truth is, I just never admitted it. I called it other things instead.

I stored so much baggage that was mislabeled and unprocessed that when I finally began opening those bags, I never knew what was going to come out. And honestly, opening some of those emotional bags felt like cleaning out a dirty attic filled with generations of junk, boxes, and forgotten trash.

Through serious pain and soul work, I finally began relabeling and processing some of that stored baggage.

Here's the story of how one realization slapped me in the face.

What I find funny now—because at the time there was absolutely nothing funny about it—is that this experience really wasn't about him at all. It was a battle between me, myself, and I, but at the time, I was convinced it was all him.

You'll see. Feel free to laugh. I do… now.

As I mentioned earlier, I met the man of my dreams—but we lived a thousand miles apart, which made things tricky. At one point, the control-freak version of me decided to travel to a city he often visited for work so we could spend time together.

Side note: controlling the relationship so I wouldn't get hurt was her (the control freak's) primary job. So I let her take over planning this trip.

There I was, sitting inside the fortress she had built. I felt safe and in control.

But when I tried to nail down the plans for this trip, he kept saying things like:

"I'm not sure yet."

"I don't know where I'll need to be that week. The only way I could commit is if I had taken time off, and I needed more notice for that."

He really did not know where he needed to be—and he said that right up until the day I left. Still, I assumed he would be there. I thought I had it all under control.

Now, you should know: in my marriage, my ex-husband did anything I asked. I equated that with love. Looking back, he was mostly appeasing the control freak in me. That had been my experience for many years, so when the new guy wouldn't commit to the trip, I thought he was just playing it cool.

When I arrived and called him to see where he was… he was in another state, with no plans to join me.

OUCH.

That hurt like (insert your own four-letter word here).

My immediate emotions were shock, followed quickly by anger.

"What the hell? I came all this way, and you're not coming?"

He calmly said, "I never said I would come. Work required me to be somewhere else this week. I've been trying to tell you that. I didn't commit because I didn't want to hurt you if I couldn't make it."

Anger burns hot and fast for me, but it dies quickly. I got past the anger easily enough, and the shock faded too. But I couldn't move on like nothing happened.

For months—yes, months—I thought about it, talked about it, journaled about it, until I could finally say the words:

"I am hurt."

For me, that was huge. I had never said it before. It felt like speaking shards of glass.

And his response?

"I'm sure that did hurt. But again, I never said I could be there. You assumed I would—I never promised that."

Okay. I'd admitted to being hurt, and I was still here.

The world did not implode.

A hole did not open up and swallow me whole.

He simply said, "Yes, I realize that hurt."

He didn't drop everything to come running. He didn't beg for forgiveness.

Meanwhile, in my head, I was thinking:

Doesn't he know I don't let anyone hurt me?

How is he so calm about this?

He flipped my whole world upside down and doesn't even know it.

Now what?

In my old world of misconceptions, the relationship obviously had to end.

He hurt me.

He didn't deny it.

More importantly—he could do it again.

So I told him I needed to move on. And the moment the words left my mouth, I knew I was making one of the biggest mistakes of my life. You know that sinking feeling when you hit send too soon on a text? Multiply that by a thousand.

It took months of reflection, journaling, and honest conversations to work through what happened. I had to learn how to forgive him for what I believed was an unforgivable offense.

But the real truth was this:

He had the ability to hurt me—when most people never got close enough to even have the chance.

And he still got another chance.

That was the slap in the face.

That's when I realized he could challenge me to grow. There was potential for a whole new level of intimacy—something I had never experienced.

I had to own my feelings and say, "Yes, I'm hurt."

Then I had to give myself permission to actually feel it—something I had never allowed before. Vulnerability and I were not exactly on speaking terms, but I knew this relationship would require those steps, and I decided it was time to take them.

I had spent my whole life treating hurt like a stop sign—something that meant I had to leave, shut down, or take control. This time, I stayed. I didn't fix it, justify it, or run from it. I just let it exist long enough to understand what it was trying to tell me.

Being hurt didn't break me or weaken me.

It became proof that I had let someone close enough to matter.

It softened me in the best way—and it allowed me to love on a whole new level.

Over time, I revisited moments in my life I had labeled as anger and realized they were actually hurt. Reclassifying them helped me heal long-standing patterns that had spilled into other relationships. Those relationships grew too.

For years, I believed that a partner who jumped through hoops to make me happy and avoided all my triggers was what I needed. In reality, it made everything worse. It created a tightrope neither of us could balance on, and the baggage piled up until the whole thing collapsed.

Hurt doesn't have to be a nasty four-letter word.

It's never fun—but it doesn't have to be feared or avoided.

It's simply part of loving deeply and being alive.

After all the layers we've peeled back, the growth we've strived for, and the boundaries we've learned to honor, we can't forget to begin each day by choosing happiness.

Choose Happy

(Hestia)

My granddad used to say, "Some days you're the windshield, and some days you're the bug."

I believe that was his way of saying we have absolutely no control over what life will throw at us today. What we can control is the disposition we put on when the day begins. We can choose happy, pissed, sad, confused, apathetic—well, we have a lot of choices.

As a child, I lived with my grandparents. It goes without saying that I had a nontraditional childhood. My parents were very young and not at all equipped to function as married adult parents. They both had very complicated childhoods of their own.

My earliest memories of "home" are of my grandparents' house. Complicated, yes—but it was my normal. My grandmother was a traditional homemaker. She cooked four-course breakfasts, three- to four-course dinners, and yeast rolls every single day for our after-dinner snack. She managed the house and everything in it. My granddad loved her deeply, completely, unwaveringly, and respectfully. It was beautiful to witness.

In addition to being a first-class husband, he was a phenomenal father figure. Not only did he teach me how a partnership should work, he was also my safety net.

He taught me to fish... with incredible patience. No matter how many times I cast my line over the telephone wire, he would shake his head, give me the "I told you to be careful" look, and trade me poles so he could untangle mine while I kept fishing.

He bought me a pony for my fifth birthday. We spent hours walking around the yard—me in the saddle navigating Dolly around trees, my swingset, and the pond. On Saturday mornings, we would saddle her up and wander until she was tired. When she was done, she'd walk me right into her barn, and my granddad would help me dismount, remove her saddle, and care for her. He taught me to brush her, feed her, make sure she had water, and to respect her.

He was always the person I went to for guidance and advice. His opinion and approval meant the world to me. He always offered guidance with honesty, respect, and love. Even when I was very young, his expectations were clear.

When I told him I was unexpectedly pregnant with my oldest, he simply said, "One mistake doesn't constitute another."
He told me that getting married just because I was pregnant would be irresponsible and that I should take time to decide what decision felt right.

When he passed, I was pregnant with my second child. We had just worked through probably the worst disagreement we had ever had, and I was crippled with guilt. That disagreement—so important in the moment—became completely insignificant compared to learning how to go on without him. I would have given my right arm for one more day with him. I still would.

I was lost. Lonely in a way I had never experienced. It felt as though I had lost the calm to my storm. Without him, I had no one to consult when I needed guidance, advice, or motivation to carry on. All of that had come from him. I felt directionless.

My sadness was bone-deep. Heavy. Like walking through knee-deep water. Everything felt exhausting. It stayed heavy for a long time. I missed him so deeply that I couldn't talk about him. Most often, just thinking of him brought me to tears.

For a long time, I struggled with guilt, anger, heartbreak, abandonment, and absolute despair.

Then one day, without thinking, I found myself saying to my husband, "My granddad used to say... How do you eat an elephant? One bite at a time."

We laughed.

That day, the pain felt a little lighter. Over time, I started remembering all the fun we had—the pony stories, the fishing stories, his singing Marty Robbins songs to me. Before I realized it, I could talk about him without tears.

The windshield and the bug remind me to choose the perspective of cherishing the time, fun, and love he gave me.

Losing him was excruciating—but he was worth every second of the pain.

I am so grateful for the relationship we had that I cherish the pain. The pain is proof that I loved him with my entire soul.

I choose to honor that relationship by choosing the perspective that I was unimaginably lucky to have this man in my life. I choose gratitude instead of abandonment. I choose admiration instead of anger. I choose to be blissfully happy that he was my granddad.

And I believe that every day, I have a choice to begin with a happy disposition. Of course, I veer off course sometimes—but that's okay. When I do, I choose to choose happy again.

Happiness is personal. No one else can define what makes me happy, and no one can make me happy.

Happiness, to me, is a feeling of bliss, contentment, and fulfillment that comes from knowing I've given my very best effort to whatever I undertake.

Those values were shaped largely by his influence. Whether I'm cleaning my toilet or caring for my children, I seek to do the best job I'm capable of. When I know in my heart that I'm genuine and giving my best, I am truly happy.

Once I figured out how to be happy and build trust with my loved ones, it became easier to find joy in everyday life. But inevitably, there are still times when I struggle to feel in control of my happiness. When that happens, I re-read a book called Psycho-Cybernetics. It's incredibly insightful and challenges the reader to apply each concept to themselves.

And I remind myself... one bite at a time.

Tomorrow, everyone has a choice.

I suggest choosing happy.

If we did our job, somewhere in these pages you laughed, you reflected, and you got at least one well-deserved smack in the face—in the best possible way. Our hope is that you keep trying out new tools, keep adding to your tool belt, and keep giving yourself room to evolve. Because life was never about becoming someone different—it's about embracing who you've always been, loving her fully, and choosing to grow with intention.

The Tool Shed

Healing requires more than just one wrench. So, we wanted to share a collection of the tools that helped us begin our journeys. One thing became very clear early on: **not every tool works the same for everyone**. Something that changed everything for one of us barely made a dent for the other.

Think of this as a starter kit. Try different tools. Keep what works. Toss what doesn't. And add your own as you go.

Here are the tools that helped us grow, heal, and (mostly) keep our sanity:

Talking to Friends

Having honest conversations—rather than turning everything into a venting session—opens the door to real support. Talking with people who can offer a different perspective, instead of just adding fuel to the fire, can help you see beyond the moment you're stuck in. Sometimes hearing how someone else interprets a situation reveals that things aren't as black-and-white as they felt inside your own head.

Books, Books... and More Books

Books saved us—in completely different ways.

Some we devoured in one sitting. Others we read one single sentence... then stared at the wall and questioned our entire life. Both experiences count.

Here are the books that made the biggest impact on us:

- **The Art of Empathy** – Karla McLaren
- **You Can Heal Your Life** – Louise Hay
- **The Untethered Soul** – Michael A. Singer

- **Daring Greatly** – Brené Brown
- **Psycho-Cybernetics** – Maxwell Maltz

We took what resonated and left what didn't. Coming back to these books at different stages of life hit differently every time.

Meditation

We were both new to it—and honestly, a little skeptical.

But guided meditations (hello, YouTube) taught us how to slow our minds, breathe, and get still enough to actually hear ourselves. It was in those slower, quieter moments that answers finally showed up.

Reiki

Athena's discovery—and a life-changing one.

Reiki helped release emotional blocks in ways she couldn't explain at the time, only feel. She found it so helpful that she eventually became certified herself. If you're open to energy work, this is a path we wholeheartedly recommend.

Journaling & Letter Burning

Sometimes it's hard to know how to start.

When we began journaling, we wrote the truth—the messy parts, and especially the things you'll never say out loud. We wrote for ourselves and to ourselves.

With letter burning, once the writing was done, the letter was burned. For Athena, the power came from saying all the things she had never said before, knowing no one would ever read them. That freedom made it possible to disregard social filters, hold nothing back, and let it all out.

There's something incredibly freeing about watching old emotions turn into ash.

Also—cry. It clears more than your tear ducts.

Counseling

Finding the right therapist is like dating—awkward at first, and sometimes you have to try a few before you find the right match.

Athena went through three counselors before finding one who truly understood her. When you find the right one, it can change everything.

Movies That Hit at the Right Time

Sometimes you don't need a book—you need a movie that mirrors your life a little too well.

For Athena, **Eat, Pray, Love** became a recurring guidepost. Every time she watched it, a different part resonated. As Julia Roberts' character reflected on her life, Athena found herself doing the same—seeing the lessons more clearly with each viewing.

Hope, on the other hand, watches and rewatches **While You Were Sleeping**. The story of a sweet, quirky loner without family pulls at her heartstrings. Sandra Bullock's character, Lucy, is wholesome and deeply relatable. We've all felt alone at times, hoping for our happily ever after. This movie offers laughs, tears, and the happiest of endings—a magical world where everything turns out right in the end. By the time the credits roll, Hope feels rejuvenated and ready to return to building her own happily ever after.

A beautiful, meaningful escape can do wonders. If you have a favorite movie, indulge when you need one. Art has a way of meeting you exactly where you are.

Music That Scratches the Itch to Feel

Whether in the car or at home, music can be a powerful catalyst for processing emotions of all kinds.

For Hope, dance—and dance music—represents the beginning of self-confidence. In high school, earning her place on a dance team helped her feel grounded and self-possessed, eventually growing into the confidence to be fully herself. Listening to energetic music still sparks that same feeling today.

Hearing **Creep** allows her to release feelings of unworthiness. **That's How Strong My Love Is** reminds her of her first true love—her son. **Ain't That a Kick in the Head** brings back memories of her grandfather singing along to his Dean Martin records. Yes... records.

If music moves you the way it moves Hope, lean into it. When you need a pick-me-up, play something upbeat. When you're working through heavier or more complicated feelings, listen to what stirs something inside you. It almost always knows what you need.

When You Come Back to This Book

This book won't read the same way twice — because you won't be the same person twice.

If you're here again, some things may feel lighter.
Some may land harder.
Some may surprise you.

This space is for noticing what changed.

You might want to jot down:

- what feels different now
- what you understand in a new way
- what you're carrying less of than before

Or you might just sit with the contrast. That counts too.

Leave a few notes for your future self if you want.

About the Authors Rene Shanti & Hope Genero

Rene and Hope are best friends who have survived multiple decades of life, love, chaos, emotional plot twists, and each other. Somewhere between late-night phone calls, questionable life choices, and a shared obsession with growth, they discovered that the only thing better than healing... is healing with someone who knows you so well they can sometimes explain yourself to you.

That kind of friendship is rare and priceless — and through this book, they hope to share pieces of that clarity, humor, and heart with you, too, so your own journey feels a little lighter and a lot less lonely.

Together, they write with honesty, humor, and heart — always hoping their hard-won lessons save someone else a little time (and maybe a little therapy).

About Hope

Hope Genero is a storyteller, empath, and boundary-builder with a tender heart and sharp intuition. Once a chronic yes-sayer, she eventually learned that "no" is a complete sentence — a lesson that shaped the foundation of her emotional work. She has spent years unlearning generational patterns, trusting her inner guidance, and becoming the grounding presence in her relationships.

Her writing blends humor, vulnerability, and perspective, helping readers see their own stories with more clarity and kindness. When she isn't writing, she's uplifting others, reflecting deeply, or offering the kind of thoughtful support that has carried her through every chapter of her life.

About Rene

Rene Shanti is a writer, seeker, and recovering "I've got this" type – even in the moments when she absolutely did not have it. Her life has included early marriage, divorce, co-parenting, trust issues, emotional excavation, and the long, imperfect process of redefining what strength truly means.

She is known for her blunt honesty, her compassion, and her willingness to call herself out before anyone else can – which is half the charm and half the chaos. Rene approaches life with creativity, humor, and relentless introspection. When she isn't writing, she's designing something, managing five projects at once, or deep-diving into her thoughts like it's a competitive sport.

www.ingramcontent.com/pod-product-compliance
Lightning Source LLC
LaVergne TN
LVHW090612110826
845146LV00001B/357

* 9 7 9 8 9 9 3 7 7 0 6 1 1 *